# THE OFFICIAL HACKER'S RULES OF TENNIS

## BY BOB ADAMS

**CONTEMPORARY BOOKS, INC.**
CHICAGO

Copyright © 1982 by Bob Adams Inc.
All rights reserved
Published by Contemporary Books, Inc.
180 North Michigan Avenue, Chicago, Illinois 60601
Manufactured in the United States of America
International Standard Book Number: 0-8092-5143-4

Published simultaneously in Canada by Beaverbooks, Ltd.
195 Allstate Parkway, Valleywood Business Park
Markham, Ontario L3R 4T8 Canada

# THE OFFICIAL HACKER'S RULES OF TENNIS

## CONTENTS

### PART ONE
### ETIQUETTE

Preparing for Battle ........................ 7
Waiting for a Court ........................ 10
How to Use Distractions ................... 12
Aggravate Your Opponent
  Early in the Match ...................... 14
Playing with the Whole Family ............. 16

### PART TWO
### DEFINITIONS

Ace ....................................... 18
Love ...................................... 18
Fifteen-Up ................................ 18
Thirty-Fifteen ............................ 18
Forty-Five ................................ 18
Ad-in ..................................... 18
Match Point ............................... 18
First Serve ............................... 20
Let ....................................... 20
Overhand Serving .......................... 20

Volley .................................... 20
Rally ..................................... 20
Singles ................................... 22
Mixed Doubles ............................. 22
Hacker's Shots ............................ 24

# PART THREE
# THE RULES

Rule 1—The Game . . . . . . . . . . . . . . . . . . . . . . 26
        Fuzzy White Spheres
        Fishing Nets
        Caged-In Area

Rule 2—Rough or Smooth? . . . . . . . . . . . . . . . 28
        When Rough
        When Smooth

Rule 3—The Sun . . . . . . . . . . . . . . . . . . . . . . . 29
        The Challenge
        The Opponent

Rule 4—Exercising . . . . . . . . . . . . . . . . . . . . . 30
        Never Before
        Seldom During

Rule 5—At Net . . . . . . . . . . . . . . . . . . . . . . . . 31
        Self-preservation
        How to hide

Rule 6—Foreign Balls . . . . . . . . . . . . . . . . . . . 32
        Entitlements
        Nearest Fence

Rule 7—Delay of Play . . . . . . . . . . . . . . . . . . . 34
        Another Martini
        Profanities

Rule 8—Playing With Spouse . . . . . . . . . . . . . 35
        Double Faulting
        Twice as Often

Rule 9—Ball Played as It Is Hit . . . . . . . . . . . . . 36
        No Exceptions
        No Allowances

Rule 10—Ball Unfit for Play . . . . . . . . . . . . . . . 38
        2 Shots
        Bouncier, Luckier

Rule 11—Sudden Death . . . . . . . . . . . . . . . . . . . 39
    When to Sweat
    When to Choke
    How to Lose

Rule 12—Disputes, Decisions & Doubts . . . . . . 40
    Cursing
    Name-calling
    Pouting

Rule 13—Superstitions . . . . . . . . . . . . . . . . . . . . 42
    Walking on Lines
    Bouncing the Ball

Rule 14—Searching for a Lost Ball . . . . . . . . . . 43
    Disrupt the Game
    Sure-fire Strategy

Rule 15—Attitude Towards
    Children on the Court . . . . . . . . . . . . . . 44
    Ping Pong
    Discouragement

Rule 16—Discontinuance of Play . . . . . . . . . . . . 46
    Never, never, never

Rule 17—Public Courts . . . . . . . . . . . . . . . . . . . 48
    When Worse Comes to Worse
    Civilized Players

Rule 18—Keeping Score . . . . . . . . . . . . . . . . . . 50
    When in Danger
    Call it "Deuce"

Rule 19—Psychological Tennis . . . . . . . . . . . . . 51
    Your Analyst
    The Consultation

Rule 20—Interference from an
    Outside Agency . . . . . . . . . . . . . . . . . . . 52
    When Disturbed
    Hot Pursuit

Rule 21—Throwing Racquet . . . . . . . . . . . . . . . 54
    Extenuating Circumstances
    Limitations

Rule 22—Ladder Matches .................56
    Bloated Egos
    Hacker's Ladder

Rule 23—Winning a Game ..................58
    Head Start
    Flying Leap

Rule 24—Proper Language ..................59
    Muffled Phrases
    Acceptable Phrases

Rule 25—Practicing .......................60
    Never, never, never

Rule 26—Television .......................62
    Drinking Beer
    Gripping Racquet

# PART FOUR
# APPENDICES

APPENDIX I—SIZING UP THE OPPONENT
    Two-hander ................63
    Terror Temper .............64
    Lobber ....................65
    Club Champ................66
    Chairman of the
      Tennis Committee ........67
    Pro........................68
    Public Court Player........69
    First-serve-acer ...........70
    Novice ....................71
    Sly-spinner ................72
    Run-around-Sue ...........73
    Racquet Thrower ..........74
    Smasher ..................75

APPENDIX II—DOUBLES
    Choosing Your Partner .......76
    In-between Shots ...........78
    Choosing Shots ............80

APPENDIX III—PROPER DRESS
    Dress for Men .............82
    Dress for Women ..........83
    Dress for Foul Weather......84
    Dress for Cold Weather .....85

APPENDIX IV—TENNIS CAMPS .........86

APPENDIX V—ROUND ROBIN .........88

APPENDIX VI—LADIES' DAY .............90

APPENDIX VII—WHEN ALL ELSE FAILS
    Switching Courts ..........92
    Feigning Injury ............93
    Dropping the Roof .........94
    Spiking the Gatorade .......95

APPENDIX VIII—SELECTING AN UMPIRE...96

# ETIQUETTE

## *Preparing for battle*

In addition to the obvious physical difficulties of spinning, twirling, speeding about and dancing around on a slippery, slinky surface to establish proper position, while at the same moment dutifully ducking and dodging the 90-mile-an-hour projectiles, the dedicated and diligent hacker must both make a saintly semblance of maintaining his poise and temperament and also make an attempt at intercepting the dangerously rocketing projectile with a crude, club-like implement called a racquet and forcefully rerouting it back over a deviously imposed obstacle called the net and into a complicated maze of lines all the while trying not to be completely outwitted by the typically clever and cunning opponent who miraculously manages to return the hacker's most carefully-planned shots and violently fires them back without any respect for the hacker's ease of returning them or his peace of mind. Whew! Tennis is clearly not a game! It is a form of war! And in order to even survive its ferocious battles, the hacker must begin by paying close attention to the pragmatic advice in this rule book.

# Good Etiquette Begins . . .

while waiting for a court. The hacker should make all efforts to alleviate boredom before the start of a tennis game.

# *How to Use Distractions!*

A hacker shall wait to serve until the opponent is thoroughly distracted and completely off-guard.

## *Aggravate your opponent early in the match!*

Treating him or her like a child is a time-proven technique for aggravating your opponent and helping to even-up the odds in a tough match. Offering careful advice in a caring and paternalistic manner will not only destroy your opponent's psyche and tennis game but will also boost the hacker's ego (which continually needs boosting). Particularly effective when playing young whipper-snappers. Doubly effective should you men-hackers be rudely challenged by the girls!

## *Finally good etiquette . . .*

means playing with the entire family at least (but hopefully not more than) once a season.

# DEFINITIONS

## Keeping Score

Ace—The times when a tennis ball flies faster than a fighter pilot ace and the hacker would only be risking life and limb to try to return it.

Love—Tennis is the only game where love means nothing.

15-Up—Not to be confused with 7-Up, this score means the hacker is off to a good start!

30-15—Time to resign yourself to defeat.

40-5—At this point nothing short of a slug from a "forty-five" will stop your opponent's lucky streak.

Deuce—Wow! You've miraculously caught up from behind and will be able to slightly delay the inevitable loss.

Match-point—Don't worry it will all be over soon!

## The Service

First Serve—High speed practice for second serve. Not expected to be playable.

Let—Abbreviation for "Pretty close serve, hacker! I'll let you take another!"

Overhead Serving—The way the pros and show-offs serve. Also used to impress the ladies while playing mixed doubles by smashing the ball into the net with tremendous force.

Double Fault—Hacker's Service.

## And If Your Serve Is Playable

Rally—The aggravating instance when the other side miraculously returns all of your best shots.

Volley—When 2 opponents lose all pretense of self-control and take viciously hard and fast shots at one another at close range.

## Some Basic Forms of the Game

Singles—The most exhausting form of tennis most often seen on TV, played by young, athletic pros.

Mixed Doubles—For the days when you have had one-too-many the night before and are not feeling up to real tennis with the boys. This aberration of the game will help occupy an otherwise vacant day.

# Mixed Doubles

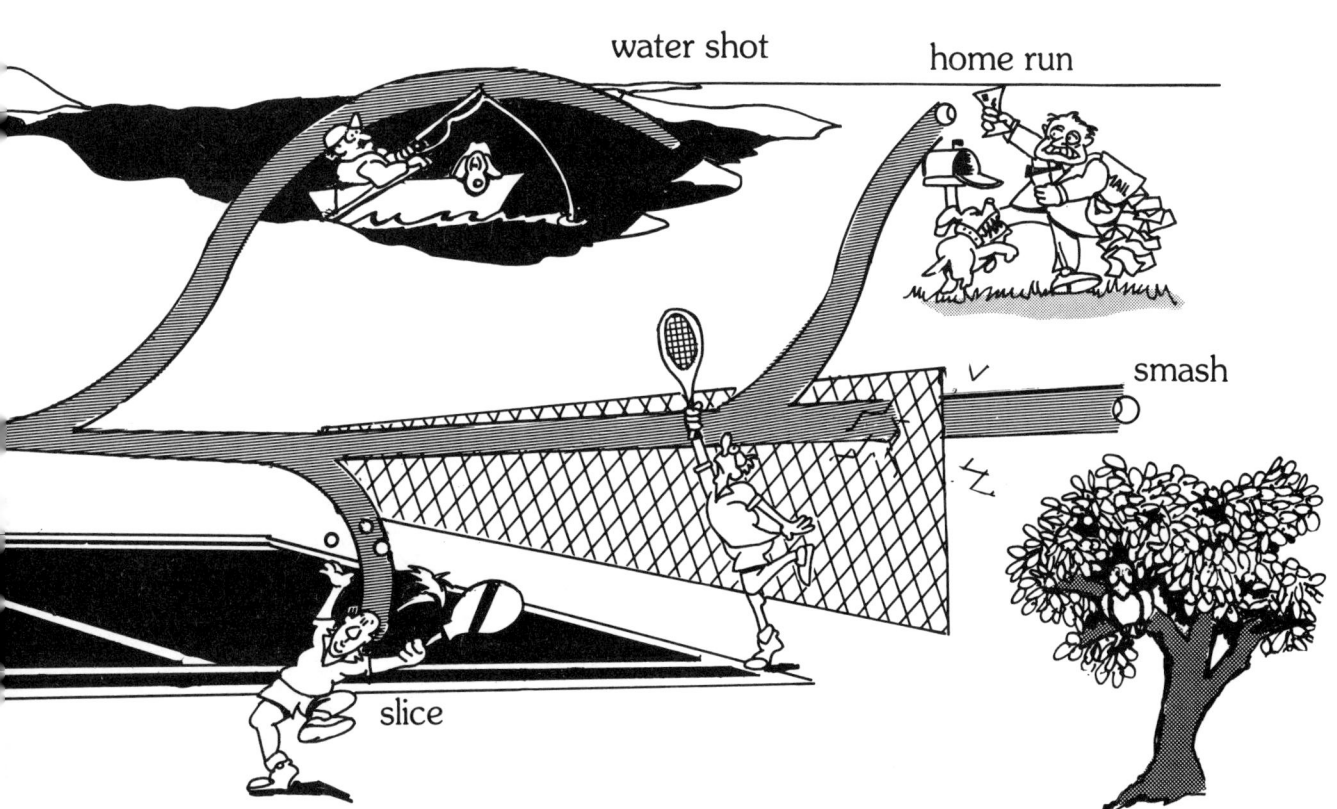

# THE RULES

**Rule 1—The Game**

*(Viewed objectively, the game of tennis is totally ridiculous, especially when the impartial observer watches four hackers attempt to hit a fuzzy white sphere back and forth for hours at a time with top-heavy, club-like implements, a task which they impede by placing what appears to be a fishing net between them and then setting themselves off from the civilized world by placing themselves inside a large caged-in area.)*

No hacker shall view the game of tennis seriously.

### Rule 2—Rough or Smooth?
When a hacker calls "rough," the racquet will always turn up smooth. When the hacker calls "smooth," the racquet will always turn up rough.

## Rule 3—The Sun

A hacker shall always allow his opponent the challenge of serving directly into the sun.

**Rule 4—Exercising**
The hacker shall never exercise before a match. And he should exercise as little as possible during the match.

**Rule 5—At Net**

When playing net the hacker's first priority shall be self-preservation! When endangered he shall either hide behind the net or shield himself with his racquet.

**Rule 6—Foreign Balls**

Anytime a hacker loses a point in the presence of a ball from a foreign court, he shall be entitled to play the point over, after hitting the wandering ball over the nearest fence.

**Rule 7—Delay of Play**

A hacker upon losing a game may pause before resuming play to:

    a) Get another martini from the clubhouse.
    b) Utter profanities at the top of his lungs.
    c) Throw his racquet into a tall tree.

## Rule 8—Playing with Spouse

A hacker shall double fault twice as often as usual when playing with the spouse.

**Rule 9—Ball Played As It Is Hit**
The hacker shall always play the ball as it is hit . . . regardless!

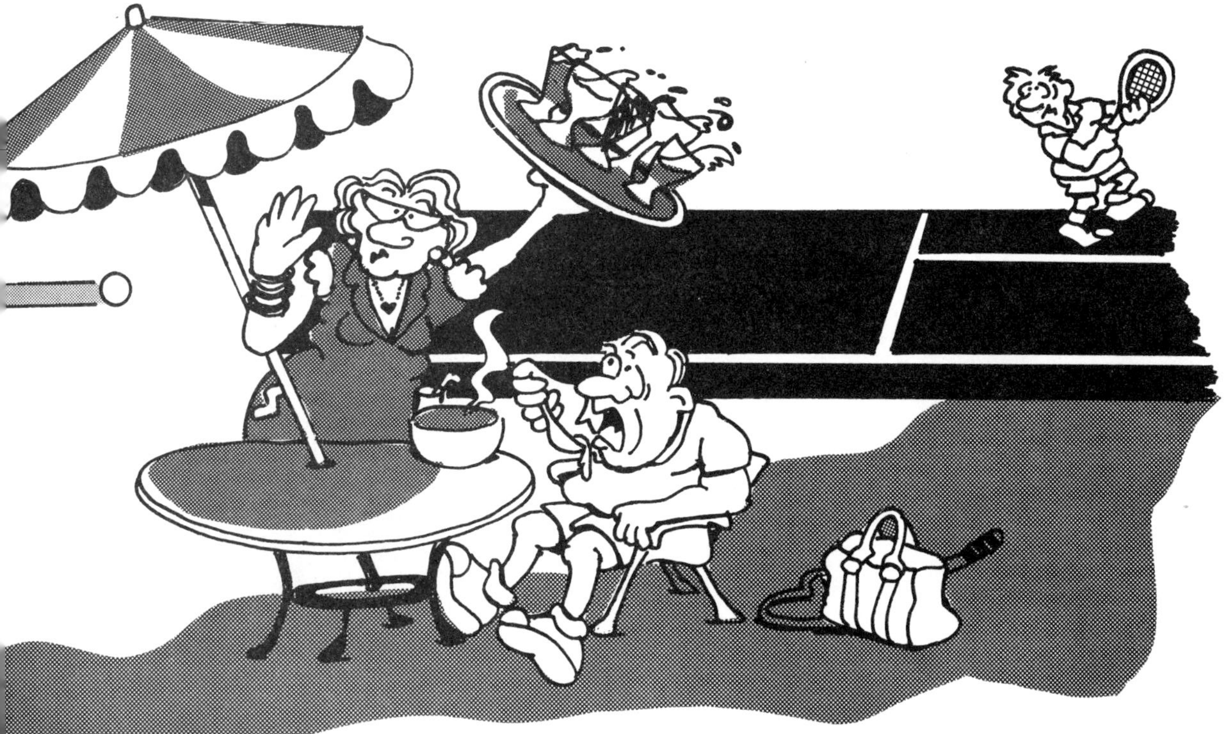

**Rule 10—Balls Unfit for Play**
The balls may be deemed unfit for play whenever two hackers shots in a row fail to clear the net. The hacker shall replace the balls with ones that are newer, bouncier, luckier and more to his liking.

**Rule 11—Sudden-death**

When a match goes into sudden-death, the hacker shall become tense and nervous; he shall sweat profusely; he shall choke completely; and he shall lose as quickly as possible. Hereafter he shall think of sudden-death as certain-death.

**Rule 12—Disputes, Decisions and Doubts**
If there be any disputes, difficult decisions or doubts that arise during a game, players shall curse, call names, shout and pout.

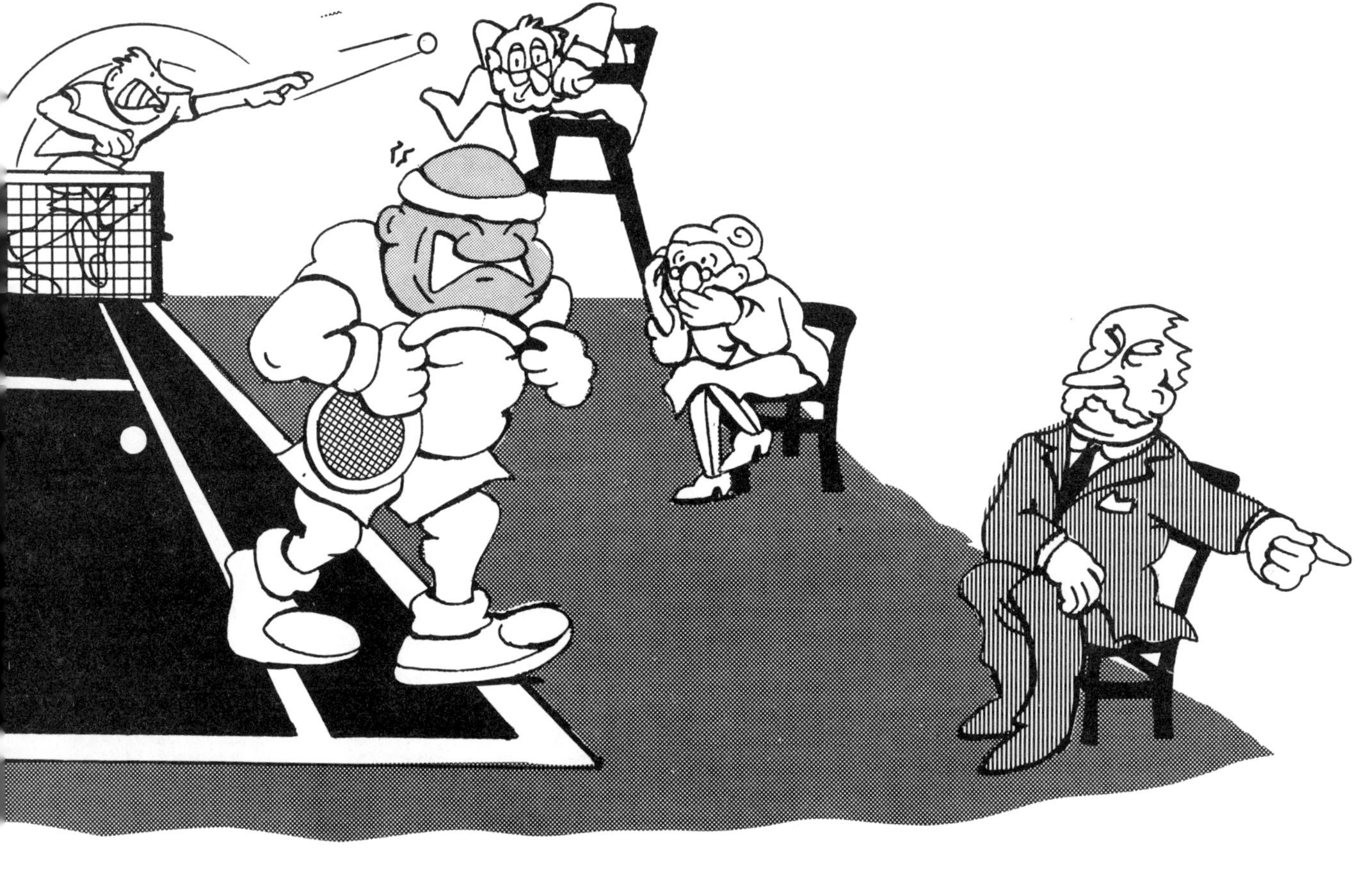

**Rule 13—Superstitions Allowed**
There shall be no rule 13. It would be unlucky. But the hacker should beware if he is foolish enough to walk on the lines or bounce a ball before service.

**Rule 14—Searching for a Lost Ball**

A search for a lost ball shall not disrupt the game unless the hacker is behind and needs the extra time to think up a new sure-fire strategy.

## Rule 15—Attitude Towards Children on the Courts

Tennis is for adults. Children should play ping pong. Any children found on a tennis court should be discouraged from the courts forevermore.

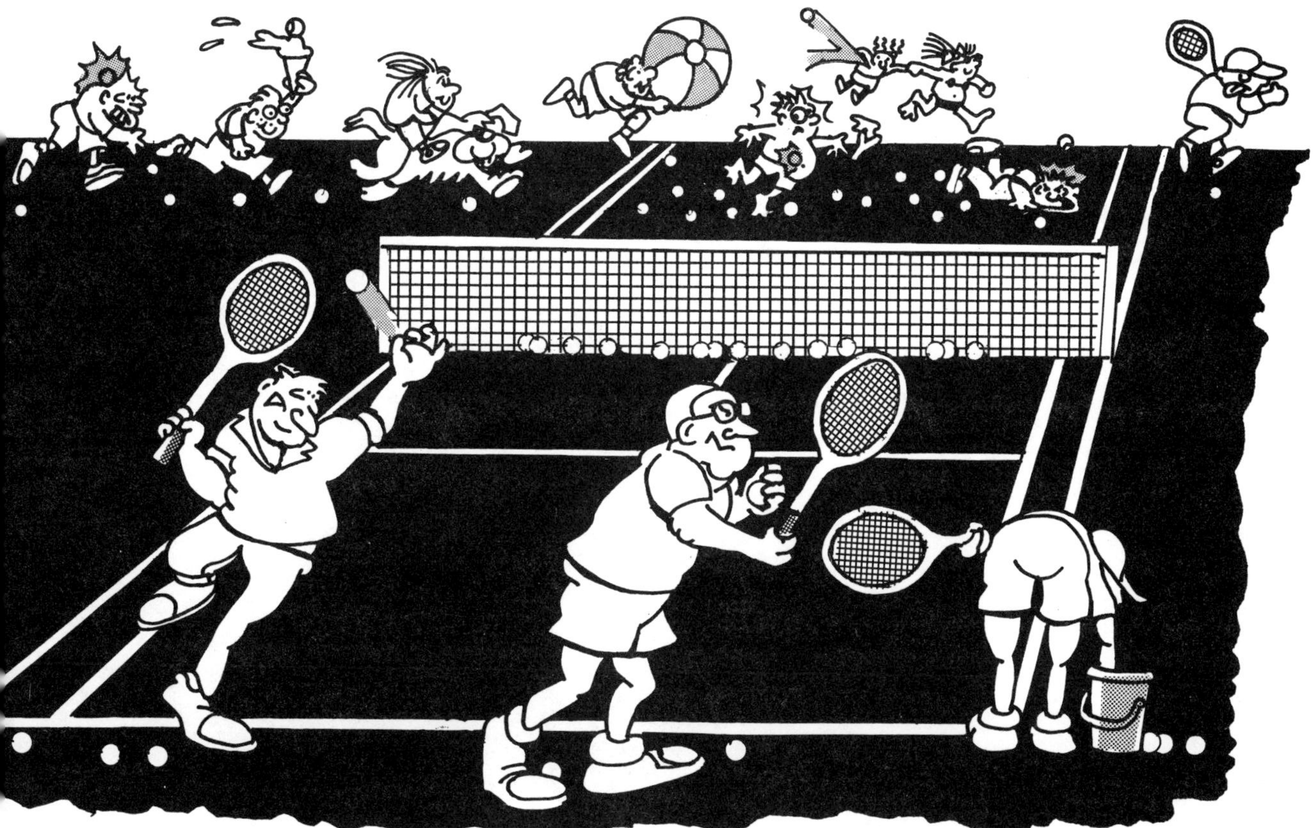

**Rule 16—Discontinuance of Play**
The hacker shall never, never, never cease playing a match of tennis under any circumstances.

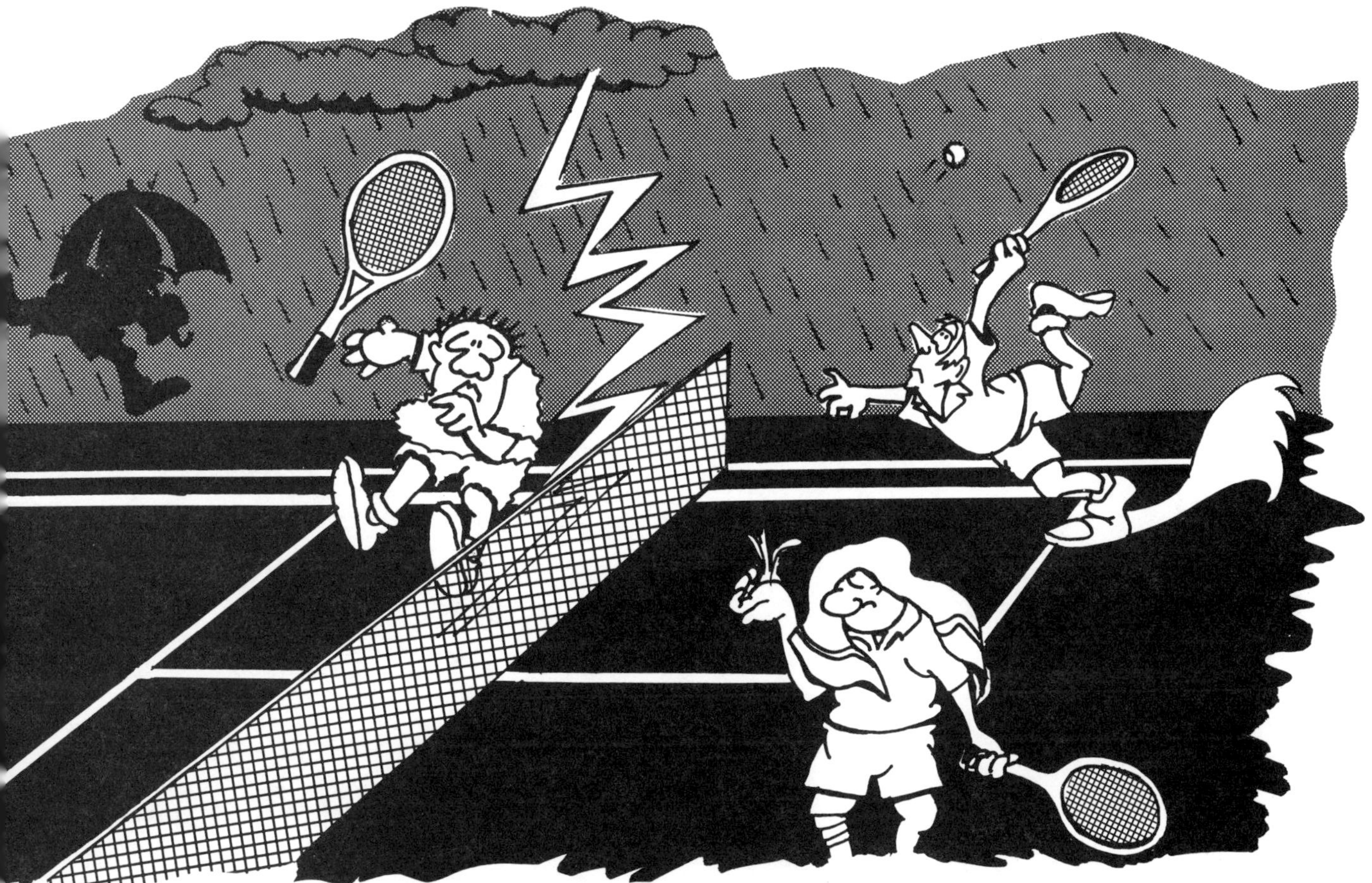

**Rule 17—Public Courts**
When worse comes to worse and the hacker is forced to play on public courts, he shall be exempt from all rules and forms of conduct normally adhered to by civilized players.

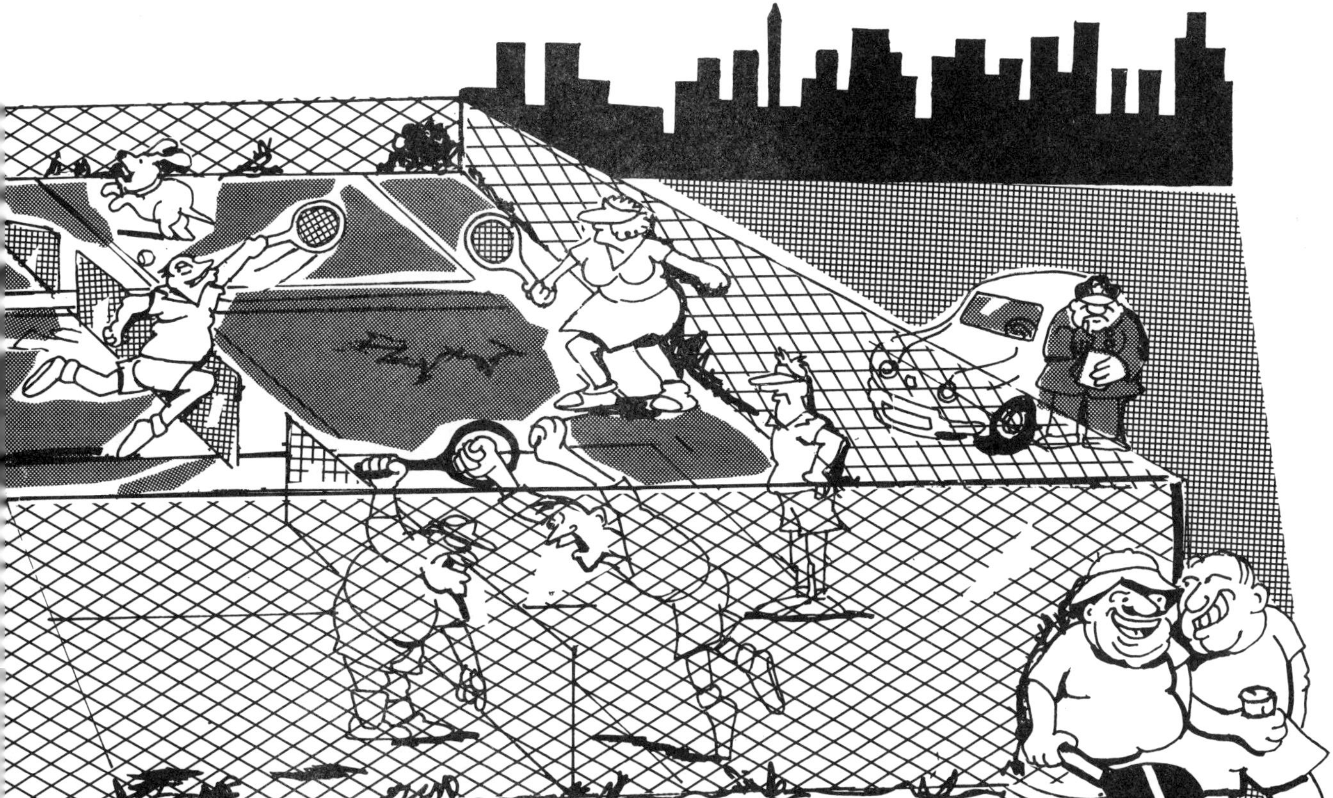

**Rule 18—Keeping Score**
A hacker shall keep careful track of the score unless he is in danger of losing, then it is always fair to suggest to call it "deuce" rather than to argue.

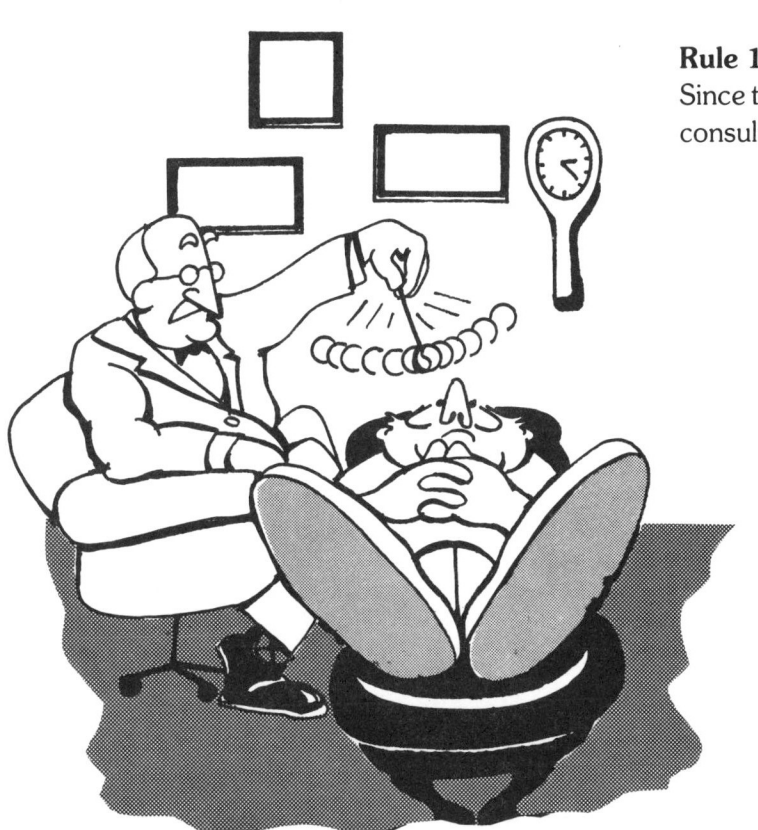

**Rule 19—Psychology**
Since tennis is a psychological sport, the hacker shall consult with his analyst on how to improve his game.

**Rule 20—Interference from an Outside Agency**
If a ball is disturbed by an outside agency the hacker shall follow in hot pursuit.

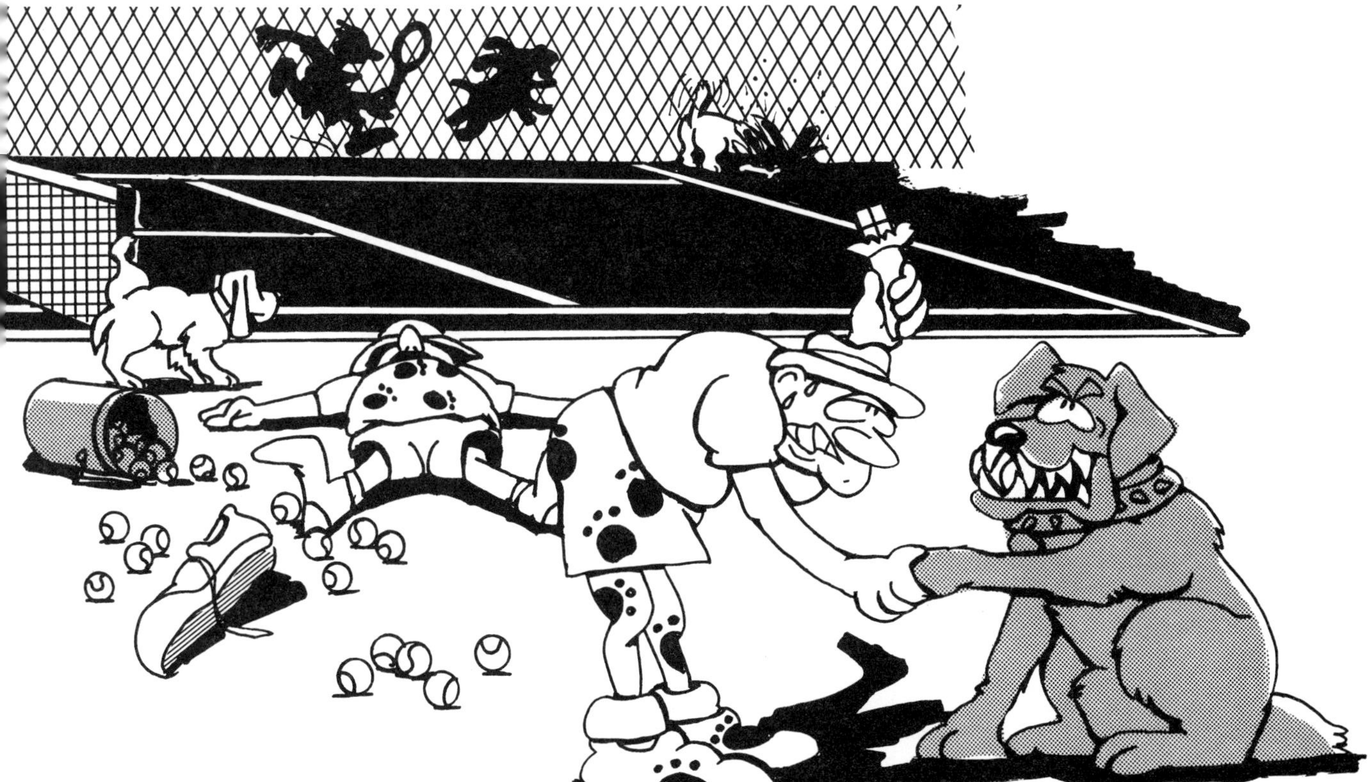

**Rule 21—Throwing Racquet**
The hacker should only throw his racquet when he feels that he can throw the racquet farther than he hit the ball.

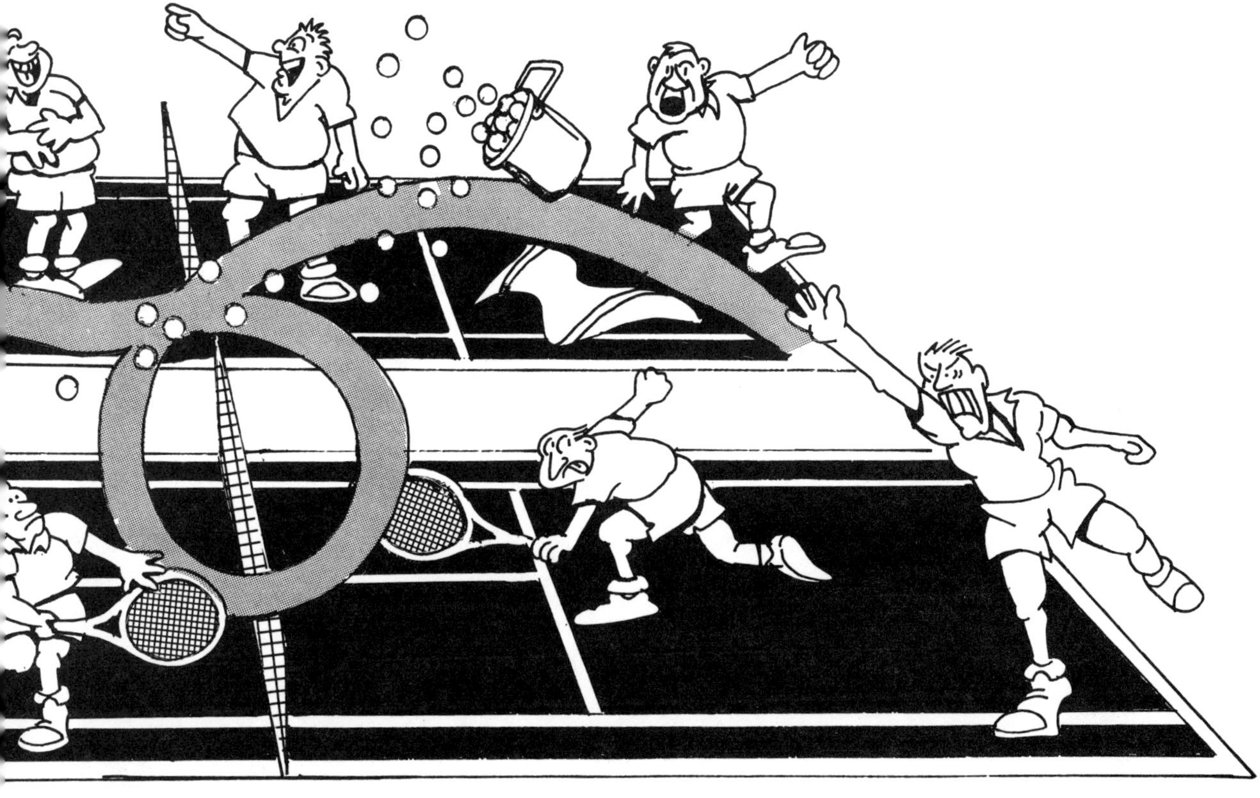

**Rule 22—Ladder Matches**

Everyone knows that tennis ladders are just designed to further inflate the bloated egos of club champs. But ironically these so-called club champs aren't really good players—in fact they always seem to lose when they are not playing ladder matches. But during the matches for ladder position they don't choke, sweat, and tense-up like all normal players do. Hence the hackers shall never take the results of ladder matches seriously.

# CLUB TENNIS LADDER

| A | B | C | HACKER |
|---|---|---|---|
| Nathaniel Exeter Hollingsworth, III | Samantha Barnard Winchester | Burno Valentino | Sam Clutz |
| Lawrence Andover Morgenthau, Jr. | Elizabeth Wellesley Butterfield | Carlos Margarita | Kate Knockover |
| Johnathan Groton Lewistall, SR. | Priscilla Smith Livingston | Paddy O'Sullivan | Fred Feeble |
| Thomas Choate Smithson IV | Patrica Holyoke Sherburne | Leroy Washington | Larry LaFault |
| Andrew Milton Woodword, JR | Virginia Brown Shephard | Chung Cheng Ching | Carol Creampuff |
| Sheldon Hotchkiss Melon II | Jackie BrynMaur | Vladimir Abramousky | Bob Adams |

**Rule 23—Winning a Game**
After winning a game the hacker shall get a running head start and then take a flying leap over the net. Every now and then he might find that one of his sneakers doesn't quite clear the net and he lands on his head—but that's one of the costs of victory.

**Rule 24—Proper Language**
Although the hacker should avoid expressing his sentiments as much as possible, an occasional muttering of the phrase sounding like "Muh-fuh-sun-beach" is perfectly acceptable.

**Rule 25—Practicing**
The hacker shall never, never practice. Remember, once a hacker, always a hacker.

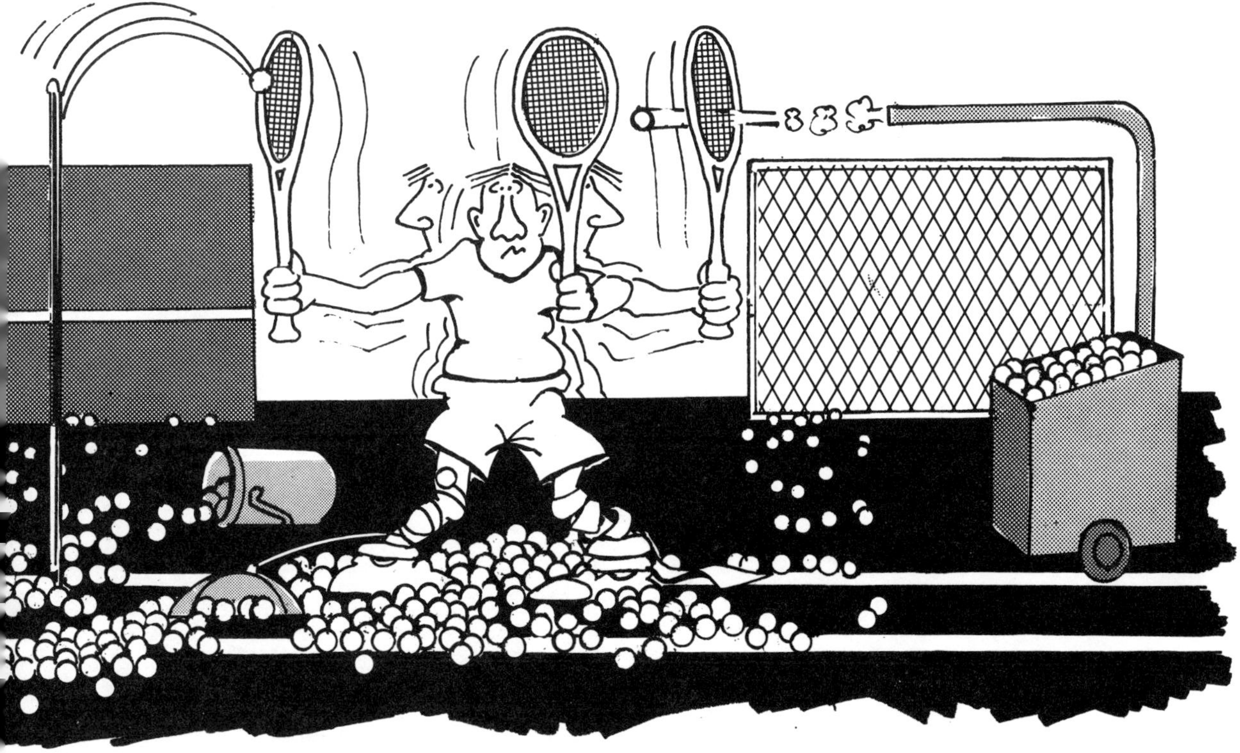

**Rule 26—TV**
A hacker shall never drink beer and hold a tennis racquet while watching TV.

# APPENDICES

## Appendix I—Sizing Up the Opponent

Especially on public courts, but even at the club, the hacker will encounter an often bewildering array of opponents—bewildering that is unless the hacker carefully studies this section of the book which will help him identify, plan strategy for and then destroy each and every opponent type.

## Two-Hander

Start in on this player (typically a female) by asking if there is something wrong with her hand. Then keep her moving on the court with wide shots that don't allow her the extra time that she requires to get into her batter-up type stance.

## The Terror Temper

Breathe a sigh of relief when you are lined up against this emotional high-wire. Almost any subtle, insightful comment you make (such as "Gee, are you sure that your racquet doesn't have a hole in it?") will break the delicate skin of this touchy player. The hacker can further fuel the Terror Temper by smiling broadly every time the hacker wins a point and by being silent when he loses one.

**The Lobber**
Invariably the lobber is constructed like his shots: big and fat. He relishes the lob because it gives him time to lazily reposition himself and collect his thoughts, while exerting the least possible amount of energy. Don't be tempted to get mad and smash the ball at him! He expects this! Instead move the ball around the court as fast as possible, tiring him out to the point where he will decide it is time to go home for a nap.

**Club Champ**

The most aggravating aspect of the club champ is that he has no particularly outstanding shot or skill at all. (Although his dress and groom is always meticulous.) He is merely a consistent, steady and non-emotional player who counts on you to make the errors. Because this player has no emotional soft spot, the hacker must use all of the tricks in the book (that is in THIS book) at once! Aggravate him by giving free advice! Play with dead balls! Turn him into the sun! Dress yourself like the public court player! Or—if worse comes to worse—join a new club!

## The Chairman of the Tennis Committee

Even before the game begins this player gives himself away by measuring the net. Then, while playing, he will constantly complain about such mundane matters as your foot faults. His apparel is always as white as the new-fallen snow, without even a colored stripe or two to brighten up his outfit or his disposition.

**The Professional**

The hacker will probably never see the professional anywhere near his club or courts but if he does, look out! A professional fires balls around the court so fast that they have been known to strike elephants dead on impact! The first warning is the cannon-like blast that occurs every time he serves, followed by a whizzing particle of white. His game resembles a real tennis game being shown on a movie screen without the accustomed pauses and in much faster motion. Stay away from this player or your ego and body will be severely damaged!

**The Public Court Player**

This player is easily identified by what he calls his tennis whites—white dungaree shorts, a dirty white T-shirt, striped socks, black basketball sneakers and a baseball cap. A six-pack of beer and a cloud of cigarette smoke follow him everywhere. Fortunately this character is usually not allowed as a guest at even the least prestigious clubs, but you are likely to encounter him should you ever have to play on the public courts. To beat this social misfit, play defensively until the beer, the smoking and the game seem to be exhausting his seldom-exercised body. Then place your shots to send him running all over the court.

**First-serve-acer**
The key to licking this young whipper-snapper is to simply hold your racquet up in the path of his service with enough strength so that the ball will bounce off your racquet and back into his court. Do not try to swing at the lightning-like service or you are sure to be aced. This player will be so surprised that you returned the service at all that his concentration will be broken and what little else there is to his game will rapidly fall apart.

**The Novice**

Even if he's having a good day this fellow is clearly distinctive from the more experienced hacker. His tennis whites are truly white without even a spec of soil, soot or sweat on them. He doesn't limp or wear a support bandage for his yet-to-be-painful tennis elbow. His arms are not yet scratched from pulling stray tennis balls out of thick bushes. But most aggravating of all, he watches the lines and carefully keeps track of the score. If this player proves to be a serious challenge, then just change the rules on him.

**The Sly Spinner**

This crafty devil has not the slightest pretension of form, style, etiquette, or good sportsmanship. He will spin every shot, serve underhanded, and always make you run! But don't despair because behind all, these dirty tricks there is only the shadow of a tennis player. So don't be lured to play in his world of lobs, smashes, spins, and other razzle dazzle. Watch his shots especially carefully as they bounce, but otherwise play a straight, hard, aggressive game. (Caution: once the tide turns in your favor watch for dubious line calls and point shaving.)

**Run Around Sue**

The obvious weakness in her backhand game makes her particularly vulnerable. Instead of forcing her to use her backhand, move her hard over to one side of the court and then fire a fast one to the far corner. (Caution: in mixed doubles keep an extra eye on her fast backcourt maneuvers.)

**The Racquet Thrower**
This notably uncouth soul is found at moments of unusually high stress at even some of the best clubs. An interesting variation with the introduction of metal is the racquet bouncer. Indeed this type has been known to bounce his racquet over the fence or even high into the trees. For either the thrower or the bouncer proceed by reminding them that the carefully calibrated torque of their racquet has been irreparably knocked out of equilibrium and the racquet will only produce erratic shots forevermore.

**The Smasher**

Typically young and unseasoned, this player has latent adolescent frustrations which he or she tries to release by smashing the defenseless, little white tennis ball—and in severe cases of "smasheritis" by trying to also bean the hacker. First defend yourself: keep the smasher as far away as possible. If caught at or near the net, dive to the ground after making your shot. Then try to give the smasher lobs to the back line—being an inconsistent player he will soon defeat himself.

**Appendix II—Doubles**

*Choosing Your Partner*

First look for worn sneakers and a few good bruises—sure signs of an experienced player. Also be sure not to select your spouse—he or she will know all of your tricks for avoiding tough shots and will probably not laugh at your jokes. Finally, choose a lefty (or a righty if you are a lefty). This way you can stay on the edge of the court and you won't have to pretend that you have a backhand.

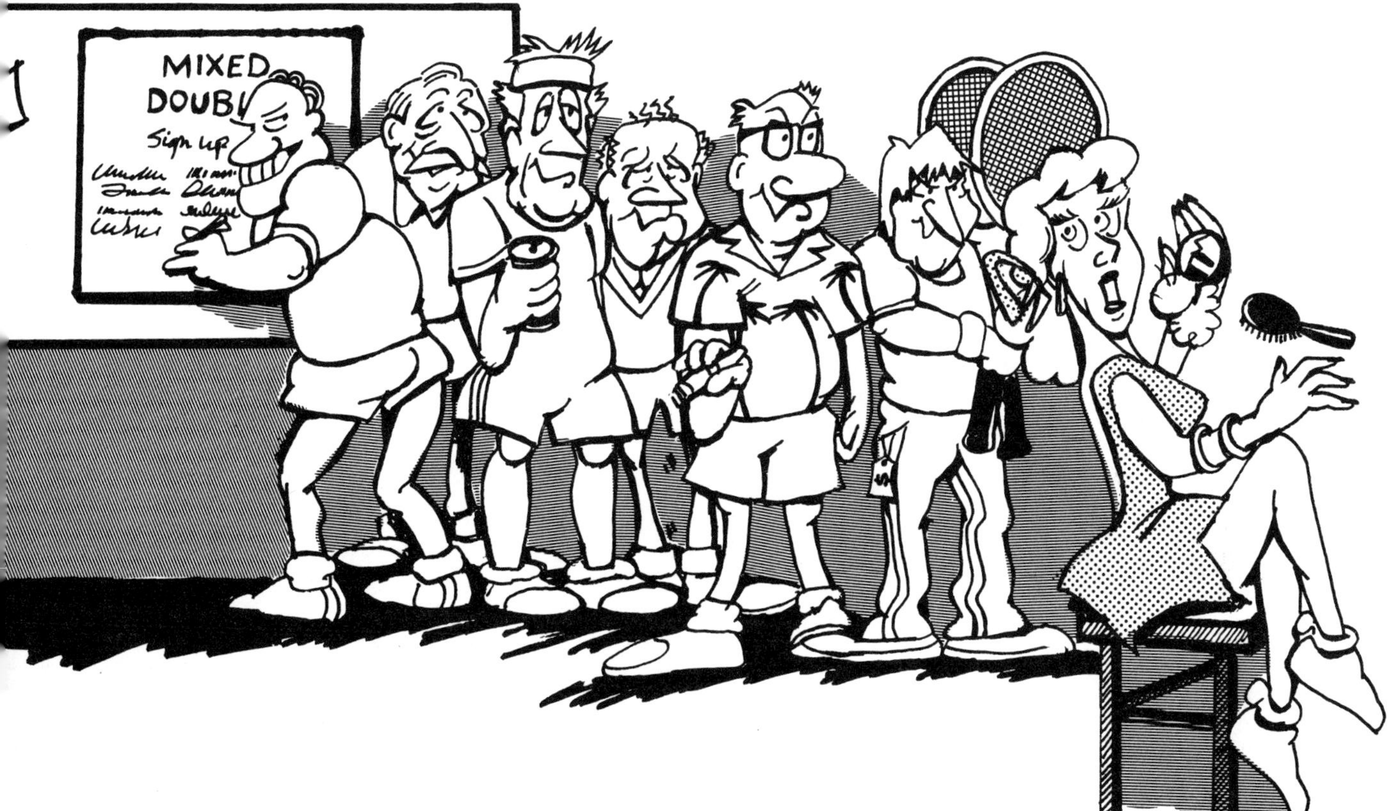
MIXED
DOUB
Sign up

*In-between Shots*

When in doubt as to who should take the shot, swing fast and hard but close your eyes and duck your head!

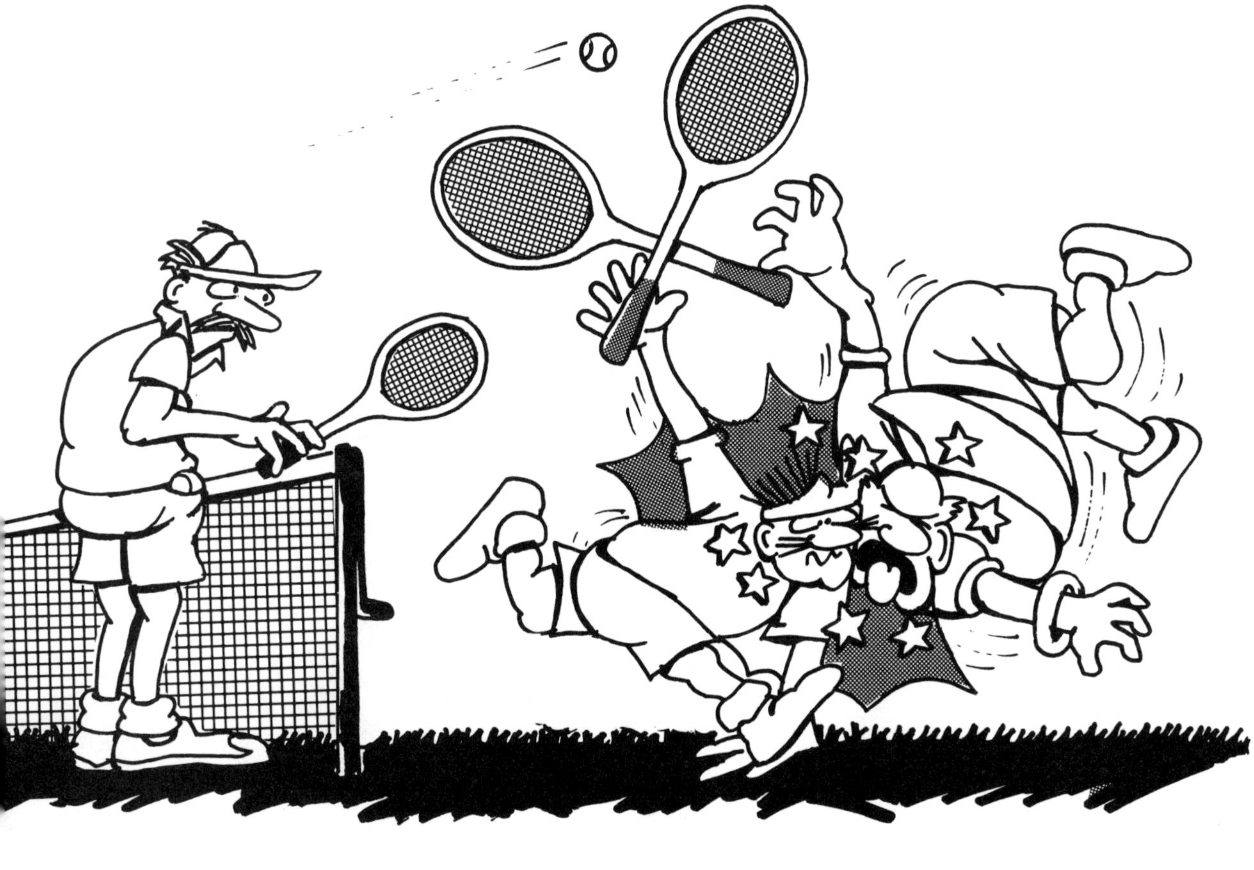

*Choosing Shots*

Let your partner return all the difficult smashes and spin shots, but take all the easy lobs for yourself.

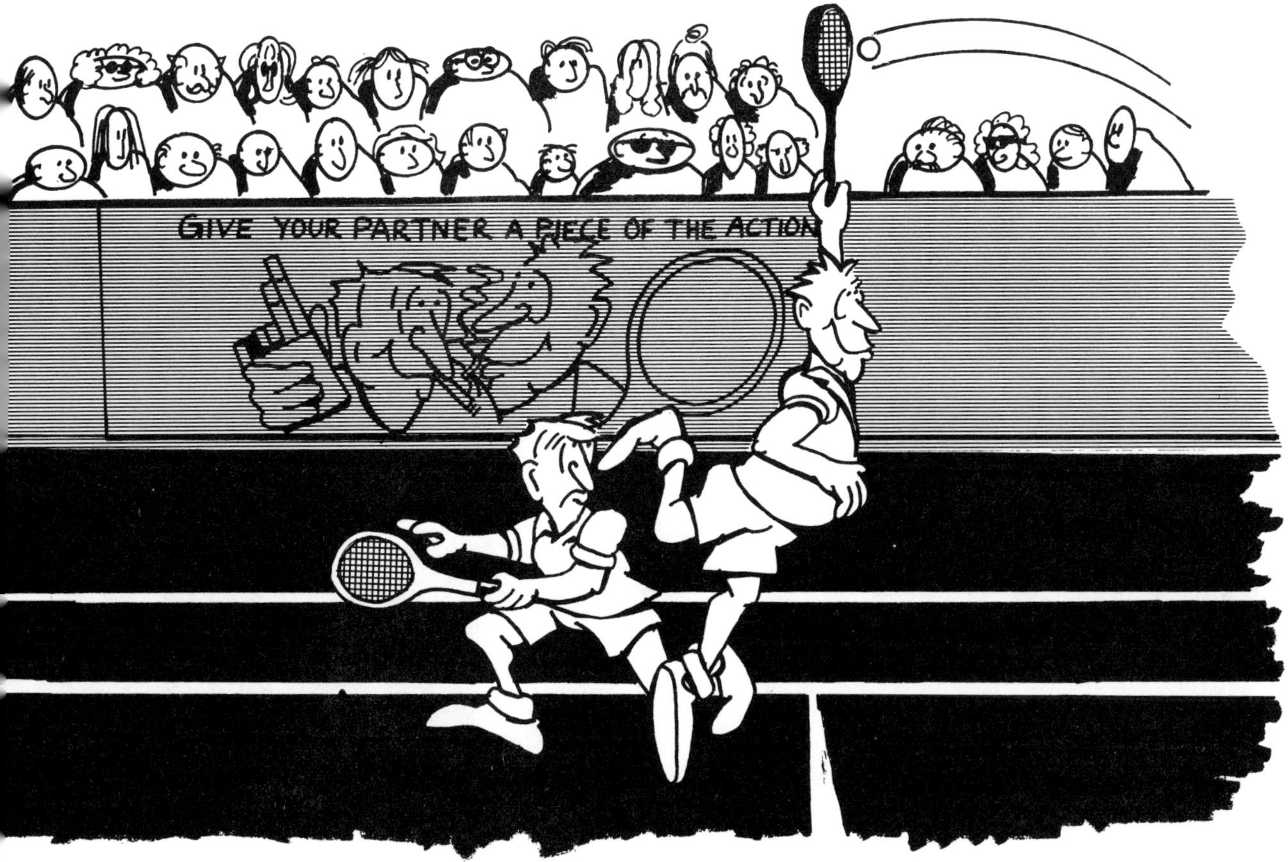
GIVE YOUR PARTNER A PIECE OF THE ACTION

## Appendix III—Proper Dress

*Dress for Men*

The main purpose of the hacker's attire is to be as inconspicuous and unobtrusive as possible. This way the hacker will be able to disappear into a crowd with his abilities (or lack thereof) more quickly forgotten between matches. Classic cream white cotton shorts and shirt are essential. If you must add a bit of uniqueness keep it simple—understated patterns are usually tolerated if visible from a distance of less than six racquet lengths. Stretched fabrics are recommended for more seasoned hackers with larger expanses to keep covered. Extra-long shirt tails are advised for novices, who are occasionally seen running on the court (and hence are more likely to show a shirt tail). A matching sweater or jacket adds the final touch of class.

## Dress for Women

A 100% cotton, sleeveless dress with a modified V-neck top and an A-line skirt provides the standard wardrobe. Some players will add a daring bright stripe (preferably red or blue) around the waist or collar.

**Dress for Foul Weather**
Skid-proof yachting shoes, a light yellow windbreaker, a big squeegee, and an umbrella-toting ball-boy are really all you need.

**Dress for Cold Weather**

A tennis mitten (with an opening for your racquet on one end and your hand on the other) and a wooden racquet (a metal one will give you frostbite if it happens to contact exposed flesh) are the first essentials. A sleeveless down jacket is the "in thing" to maximize warmth without dampening arm movement. Add a fluorescent orange (so you don't get run over by a snowplow) warm-up suit and your outfit is complete.

**Appendix IV—Tennis Camps**
Since tennis camps will turn the most mellow, happy, loving, naive, enjoyable but losing hacker into an aggressive, mean, tough, serious, depressed, egotistical, but winning player, all hackers shall never go near a tennis camp except to rescue their kin.

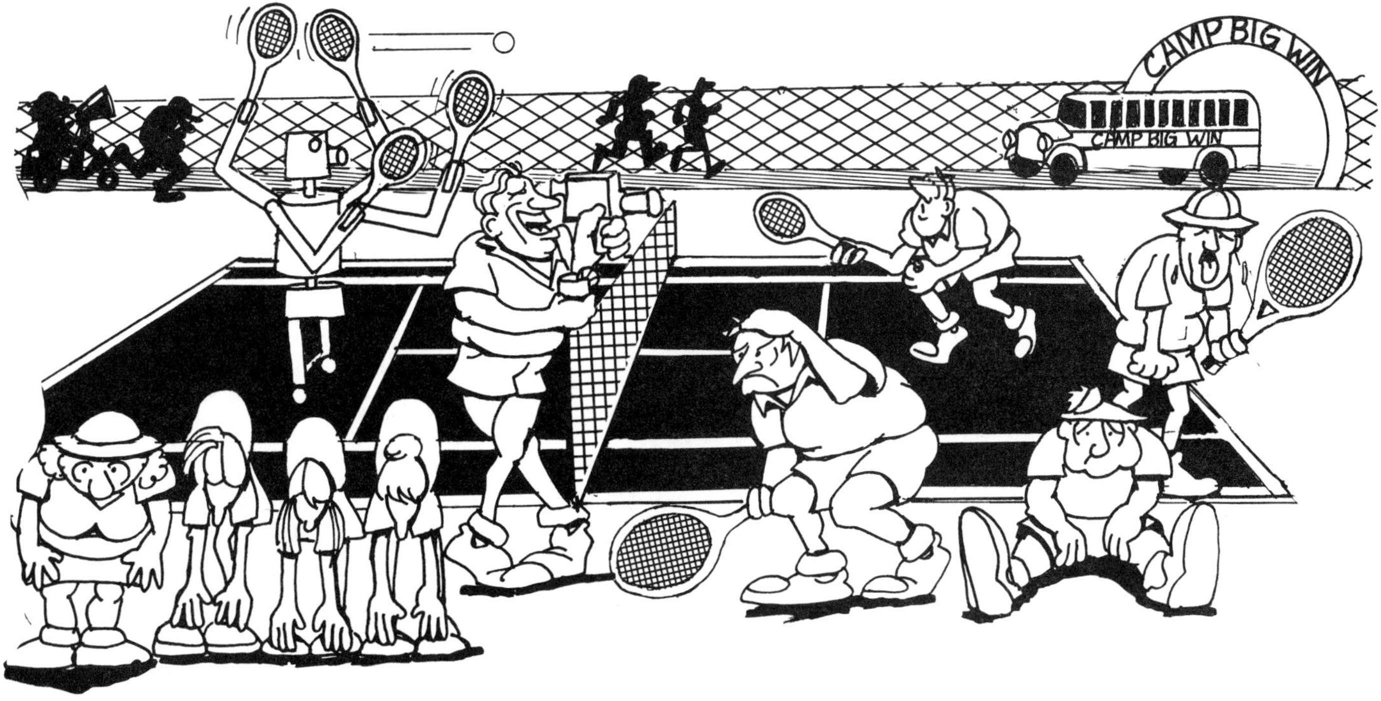
CAMP BIG WIN
CAMP BIG WIN

**Appendix V—Round Robin**

The nice thing about a round robin is you never know who is coming around next . . . But how come all the hot-shots seem to turn out for these events?

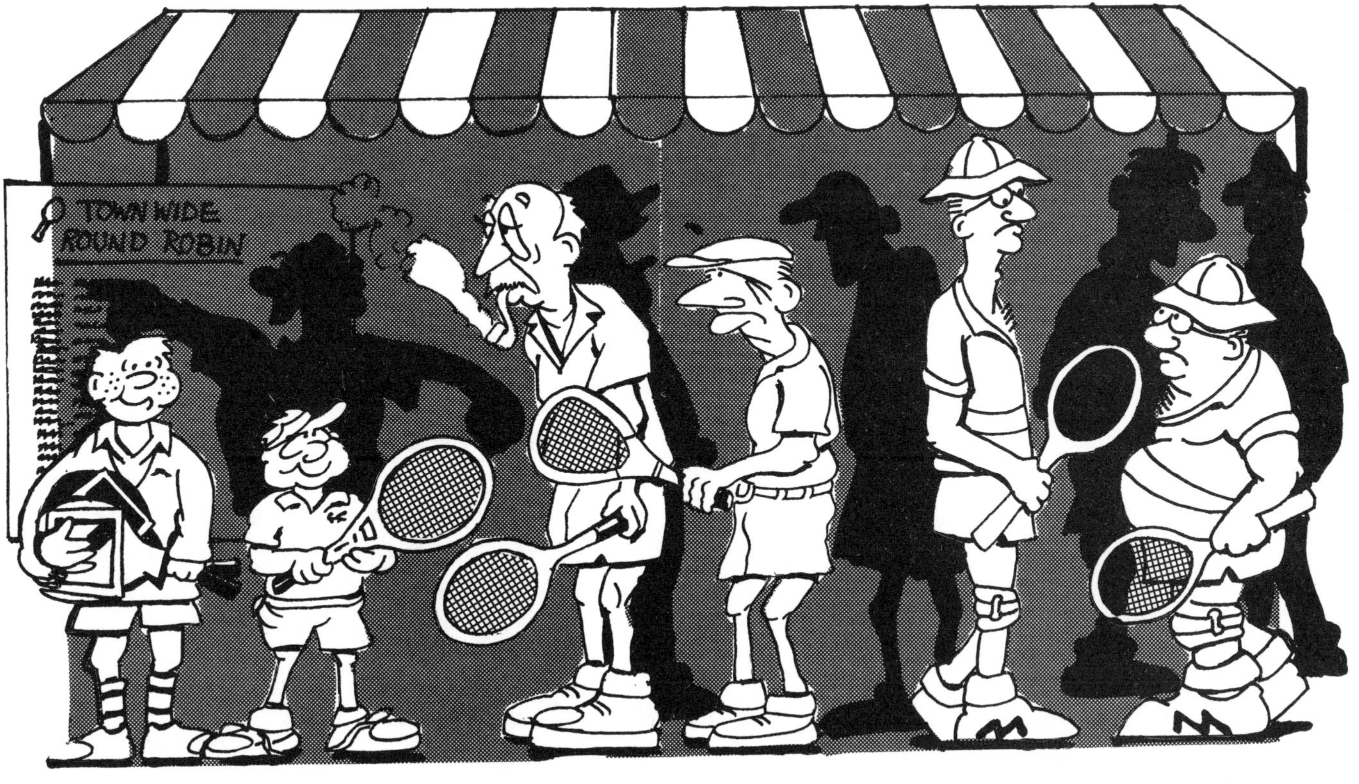
TOWN WIDE
ROUND ROBIN

## Appendix VI—Ladies' Day on the Courts
On Ladies' Day there shall be only one rule: no men.

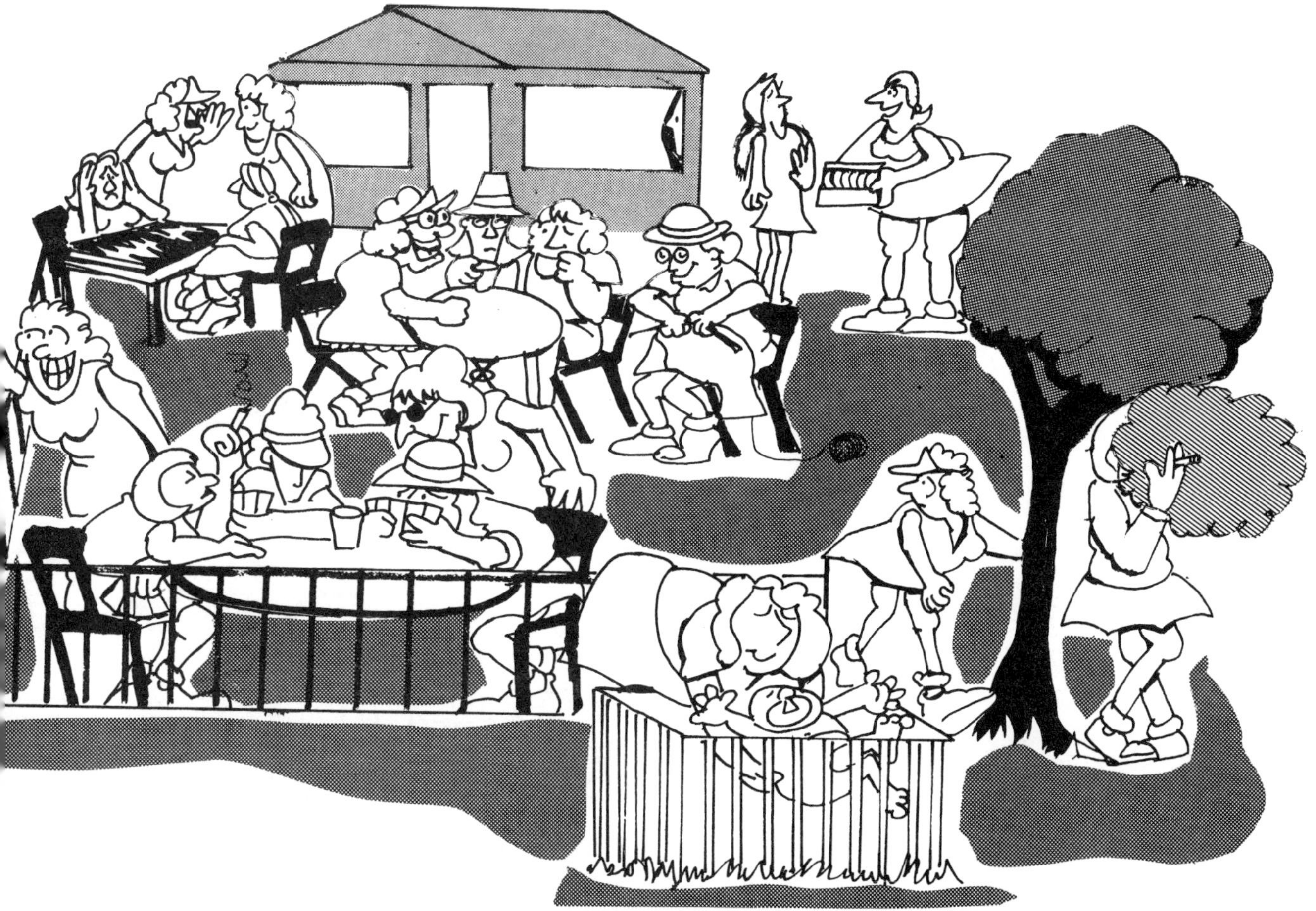

**Appendix VIII—When All Else Fails . . .**
The hacker shall suggest that play be switched from the club's clay court to a public hard-surface court. If the hacker is still in danger of losing, he shall suggest that play be continued on his great-grandfather's private grass court.

**When all else fails . . .**
the hacker shall feign injury rather than lose an important club match.

**When all else fails . . .**
the hacker shall arrange to have a confederate drop the bubble roof over the indoor court.

**When all else fails . . .**
the hacker shall spike the Gatorade with vodka and gin.

**Appendix VIII—Selecting an Umpire**

Since a hacker will probably do everything else wrong, he or she must be particularly careful to select the proper umpire. The hacker shall choose an umpire that is near-sighted, partially deaf and, most importantly, the umpire shall be perched out of racquet-reach!